How Animals
Live Together

By the Same Author

The Amazing Dandelion
The Apple and Other Fruits
Bulbs, Corms, and Such
The Carrot and Other Root Vegetables
The Courtship of Animals
The Harlequin Moth
How Animals Tell Time
How to Grow House Plants
The Language of Animals
Maple Tree
Microbes at Work
Mimosa, the Sensitive Plant
Peanut
The Plants We Eat
Play with Plants
(*Newly Revised Edition*)
Play with Seeds
Play with Trees
Popcorn
The Tomato and Other Fruit Vegetables
Vegetables from Stems and Leaves

Millicent E. Selsam

HOW ANIMALS LIVE TOGETHER

Newly Revised Edition

illustrated with photographs

William Morrow and Company | New York 1979

Library of Congress Cataloging in Publication Data

Selsam, Millicent Ellis, 1912-
  How animals live together.

  Bibliography: p.
  Includes index.
  Summary: Discusses social relationships among animals, particularly within the same family.
  1. Animal societies—Juvenile literature. [1. Animal societies] I. Title.
QL775.S44 1979   591.5'24   79-13308
ISBN 0-688-22212-9
ISBN 0-688-32212-3 lib. bdg.

Printed in the United States of America.
1   2   3   4   5   6   7   8   9   10

Acknowledgments for Photographs

American Museum of Natural History, 23, 47, 51, 59, 69, 70
Bruce Colman, Inc.: Jen and Des Bartlett, 19; Norman Meyers, 22; Leonard Lee Rue III, 20, 25, 40, 53; George B. Schaller, 65
East African Wildlife Society, 55, 57
National Geographic Society, Baron van Lawick, 10, 63
New York Zoological Society, 18, 34, 49, 56
Photo Researchers, Inc.: Jen and Des Bartlett, 45; Hugh Halliday, 27; Robert C. Hermes, 61; Joe Munroe, 38; National Audubon Society Collection: Lynwood M. Chase, 83, 85; Stephen Dalton, 75, 78; Treat Davidson, 77; Eric Hosking, 32; Lee Jenkins, 31; Jeanne White, 16, 42
George B. Schaller, 11
United States Department of Agriculture, 29, 67

The author wishes to thank
Dr. John P. Scott
of the Center for Research on Social Behavior,
Bowling Green State University,
for reading the manuscript of this book.

Contents

1 | The Sociable Animal World 9

2 | Togetherness in Animals 14

3 | Peck Orders in Birds 37

4 | The Social Life of Mammals 44

5 | Insect Societies 73

Bibliography 89

Index 93

·1·

The Sociable
Animal World

The animal world is sociable. There are words like *schools* of fish, *flocks* of birds, *herds* of deer, *packs* of wolves, *troops* of monkeys and apes, and *colonies* of insects to describe the different social groups of animals.

For a long time, all that was known about the social life of animals came from stories told by woodsmen, Indians, trappers, and hunters. Much of this information was interesting, but not all of it was reliable. For accurate knowledge about the social life of animals we now turn to the scientists who have spent weeks, months, and even years in forests and fields, watching the daily life of animals. Equipped with

9

Jane Goodall watching chimpanzees

binoculars, cameras, and notebooks, these researchers record exactly what they see.

A number of especially valuable studies have been carried out in the 1960's and 1970's. Among them are Iain Douglas-Hamilton's work on elephants in Tanzania, George Schaller's on the mountain gorilla in the Congo and Tanzania, and Jane Goodall's on wild chimpanzees on the shores of

Lake Tanganyika. During this period there has been a great
increase in such field studies, and today we know much more
about the social behavior of animals in the wild than we
did twenty years ago.

Anyone who has been around wild animals knows how
hard it is to get near them. An animal is always watching
to prevent enemies from taking it by surprise. For this reason, scientists have had to find ways to hide from the animals so that they would go on with their ordinary activities
undisturbed. An observer sometimes stays far enough away
to look through binoculars. He can get closer if he builds a
hide, a little hut of some kind that blends into the scenery.
He might sit up in a tree for hours if this perch gives him

George Schaller watching lions

a good view. Or he can follow herds of moving animals in a Land-Rover, on horseback, or on foot if necessary.

The technique used depends on the kind of animal being observed. Sometimes the investigator allows the animals to get used to his or her presence until they pay no attention and behave in a normal way.

Besides field studies, much work has been done on the social life of animals in zoos and laboratories. Some zoos have imitated the natural surroundings of an animal by putting in rocks, caves, or trees to make the animal feel at home. Some work has been done with animals kept in cages. These studies have given us very valuable information, for in such places experiments can be planned and carried out. But many animals change a great deal when kept in captivity, and the results of such studies have to be checked with observations made in the field.

In the long history of life on Earth, animals have developed amazing social relationships. There are social hierarchies in which one animal bosses another, which bosses another, and so on down to the lowliest member of the society. In other animal groups the animals associate on a free and equal basis. In some societies all members follow the leader. Still other groups are very complicated communities in which the jobs are done by animals that may even look different from each other.

The chapters that follow show what goes on among the

members of a flock of chickens or pigeons, and among the thousands of birds in a vast breeding colony. The social life of monkeys and apes is explored. We find out which sheep follows which in a flock, and which deer leads a herd. All the information reported here is based on the long, careful, and painstaking research of many devoted scientists.

·2·

Togetherness in Animals

A famous biologist, W. C. Allee, began his work on the social life of animals when he was a graduate student. He was studying some small animals called isopods that lived in freshwater streams, and he noticed that they had a peculiar habit of piling together in clusters. Where there was one animal, others soon collected. This behavior became a challenge to him, and he determined to find out the cause. One thing led to another, and he spent the rest of his life investigating the group behavior of many animals. Allee is one of numerous scientists who have studied the social habits of animals.

Even the lowliest living things, single-celled animals called protozoa, are attracted to each other. For example, the paramecium, a protozoan that lives in fresh water, is attracted by the slightly acid chemicals given off by another paramecium. Others enter the area and are attracted, and soon there is a crowd of paramecia.

Great masses of animals sometimes gather simply by accident. They may be blown together by the wind or carried together by tidal currents or waves. Miles of water in the sea sometimes become covered with a red, brown, or green bloom due to millions of microscopic organisms. If you ride in a boat on a warm summer day, you may pass thousands of pale moon jellyfish drifting in the water. Or the sea may become brilliant with phosphorescence where teeming billions of a protozoan, *Noctiluca,* are brought close to shore by the crashing waves. Other crowds of animals, such as Mayflies, may collect in response to light. Something new is added to gatherings of animals, however, when the animals are attracted to each other and stay together for a time.

Do animals derive any benefits from living together? Some scientists decided to test this question by separating fish that usually grew up in groups. They took several eggs from a batch in one aquarium, and put each egg in a separate dish. The rest of the eggs were left together. The results were amazing. Most of the separate eggs failed to hatch, or if they did hatch, the young fish soon died. Those

goldfish

eggs that were kept together hatched out into young fish that grew normally. When the young fish were separated, they soon died. The reason is still unknown, but many experiments are being done to find out whether eggs and young fish give off a chemical that helps the growth process.

Goldfish grow faster in water in which other goldfish have lived than they do in perfectly clean water. Here again it is possible that the fish give off a chemical that stimulates growth. W. C. Allee thought of another possibility. He noticed that goldfish often regurgitate extra food they have eaten. This food is in the tank when the new fish are put in and serves as an additional food supply, which could account for the extra growth.

It is interesting, too, that fish in a group eat more than they do when alone. They imitate each other. If one fish starts to feed the others join in, even if they have just finished a big meal. Fish in a group may grow more because of this habit.

Fish protect themselves better in groups also. If a certain amount of poison is put into water containing one goldfish, it will die quickly. But if the same amount of poison is put into the same amount of water with a group of ten goldfish, the fish survive for a much longer time. One of the reasons may be that fish secrete a slimy mucus into the water. This slime somehow changes the poison so that it is not as harmful, which can be a great advantage to fish in ponds, lakes, and streams. If a poisonous material accidentally gets into the water, fish living in groups may survive long enough for the poison to settle to the bottom or run off. In such a case, the fish in a group might recover from a disaster that would be fatal to a single fish.

We know that about 4,000 kinds of fish school with their own kind. Schools of herring, minnows, mackerel, and other fish move together through the sea. There may be only a few fish in a school or millions of fish. Usually all the members of a school are the same size, and usually each fish swims a definite distance apart from the next fish. From

school of Atlantic mackerel

the experiments above, we know that they will feed more and stay healthier together. But there is one great disadvantage: when a larger fish comes along it will find a whole school of fish to feed on. And fish in schools have no advantage at all when men come along in fishing boats with large nets and scoop them all in.

Defense Together

There still may be safety in numbers, for then there are many eyes to perceive the danger of attack. When a school of fish is attacked by a big fish, it breaks up and each darts away in a different direction. Some scientists think that this response may tend to confuse the predator.

Other kinds of fish may confuse the predator in a different way. They may swim down into the mud and stir it up or move around rapidly, making bubbles that help to hide them.

Schools of fish also may protect themselves in still another way. When a member of a school of minnows is injured, it releases an "alarm" substance into the water. This substance causes other fish to scatter and move away from the danger zone.

Starlings flying together in flocks can defend themselves better against predators. When they are above a hawk they fly in a loose formation, but if a hawk should fly above them, they gather together into a tight flock. This close formation can prevent the hawk from striking one bird with its sharp talons. It has also been shown that starlings can mob the hawks that attack them. Together, they can actually chase a hawk until it goes away.

Killer whales join together to defend themselves and can beat off an attack this way. A report from the research

killer whales (male on left)

ship *Calypso* tells how it chased a school of killer whales. The school consisted of seven or eight females, about seven calves, and a single large male. At first the whales dived every three or four minutes and surfaced a half mile away. A small boat from the *Calypso* followed them. Then the whales began to zigzag in front of the boat. The male and one large female remained visible while the rest of the school escaped in an opposite direction.

Musk oxen are famous for their defense tactics. In one account, several oxen together faced two wolves on the attack. The rest of the herd lay down behind them. But

musk oxen in defensive circle

then one wolf circled around toward the rear where a calf was grazing. The calf ran to the center of the herd, and all the resting oxen rose to their feet. At this point the wolves left the area.

Many ants and termites have a "soldier" caste whose main role is to defend the colony. They also have "alarm" chemicals that signal danger. These chemicals, called "pheromones," may cause the insects either to run toward the danger area and join the battle or to scatter.

Red deer rest together in a circle facing outward. In this way, they keep a lookout in all directions. They also bark when a predator approaches, which signals the herd to move off.

In chacma and yellow baboon troops, there are usually some males watching while the rest feed. If a predator approaches, the males bark a warning. If the predator does not go away, the troop will retreat while the males cover the rear.

Feeding Together

White pelicans wait in a line along the beach until the tide comes in, bringing with it many fish. Then they glide out to sea together and, at a certain distance, form into a line facing the beach. Together they move forward, plunging in the water as they go, driving the fish before them in to shore.

Starlings in flocks also can find food more easily, because

white pelicans

the more experienced birds lead the way to the feeding area. While they search the fields and meadows together for insects, each bird moves rapidly over the ground, spurred on by the others. If one misses an insect, the bird behind is sure to get it. The group as a whole can stir up more insects than a single bird.

Wood pigeons together in a flock collect food faster than single birds do. Scientists watching them have found that single birds spend more time looking around to protect themselves against predators.

Many mammals hunt together in groups. Packs of killer whales hunt schools of porpoises. They form a large circle around them, then gradually draw together. One whale at a time moves in and eats several porpoises until they are all gone.

Lions hunt together too. When they sight a herd of antelope, they fan out and then slowly move toward the herd. When close to the prey, they rush toward it from different directions. Several lions together are twice as successful as a single lion, and they also can bring down much larger prey such as giraffes and water buffalo.

Wolves hunt in packs. If a small animal is being chased, only one or two members of the pack join in. But when a large animal like a moose is being chased, ten or more members of the pack work together.

African wild dogs and hyenas go after gazelles and zebras by running together as fast as they can. If a gazelle or

African wild dog

zebra circles back, the dogs in the rear of the pack fan out to catch it. Together the pack tears the prey to pieces.

Chimpanzees yell, scream, beat on tree trunks, run around, bark, whoop, and cry when they discover a fruit tree full of ripe fruit. They make so much noise that other members of their group can find them by running in the direction of the sound.

Company at Night

Gathering darkness brings many birds together in "sleeping parties." John K. Terres, in his book *The Wonders I See,* tells of one summer evening when he and his wife were sitting in their garden. They began to hear the screech-like notes of many American robins overhead. They followed the birds to a roost in a street lined with tall pin oaks and found that more than just robins were gathered there. Grackles and starlings shared the trees with them. Another night Mr. and Mrs. Terres watched the birds stream in to this roosting area. At 6:30 P.M. the starlings came. Then grackles arrived in large flocks, and just before dark the robins. They counted the number of robins and estimated that 60 appeared every minute. Multiplying this rate by the number of minutes the robins continued to arrive, they estimated that there must have been between 3000 and 4000 robins settling down in the trees for the night. With them were about 6000 starlings and 6000 grackles.

a gathering of starlings

In New York City in the autumn starlings roost on the iron scaffolding under the 125th Street viaduct. Thousands of them stream in from all directions at sunset.

In tropical jungles parakeets feed all day in the high tree-tops. But toward evening they rise and fly together to one tall tree. Several hundred birds gather there as a temporary stopping place, and then together they dart into the air and circle around. Suddenly they descend into a tree near a bamboo thicket and, after a few minutes, dive into the bamboos for the night.

Perhaps birds keep warm by crowding together at night. Maybe they find safety in numbers. Or perhaps they just have an urge to be together.

Migrating Together

Birds and other animals that migrate to warmer climates during the winter seek company also. Crows, waxwings, bobolinks, blackbirds, kingbirds, geese, ducks, and many other birds gather together before they sweep south. A few, like Canada geese, travel in family parties, but most do not. Young birds may take off together before the parents leave, or the older birds may leave first. In any case, most birds travel south in groups.

Monarch butterflies live solitary lives till the summer comes to a close—then they become sociable. They leave the fields, and one by one drop down close to another butterfly until bunches have gathered on trees and bushes. Then they start south. Those from the Northeast of America fly to Florida, those from the Midwest go to Mexico, and those from the Pacific Northwest go to the Monterey Peninsula of California. On their way south thousands stream along together. At night they come to rest in tall evergreen trees, and so many of them land in each tree that they practically cover the leaves with their black-and-orange wings.

monarch butterflies wintering in California

This sleeping together helps to protect them from butterfly-eating birds. Monarchs produce disagreeable-tasting secretions, and at night the odor of many individuals collected together helps to keep their enemies away. Chilled by the cold, the monarchs stay quiet and still all through the night, but in the morning the sun warms them and they continue the flight south.

Many sea mammals such as dolphins and whales travel together in schools. They usually move to cold polar regions in the spring and back to warmer waters in the fall. One of the whales, the humpback, is noted for its songs—a long series of squeaky eerie notes, which they can repeat over and over again. These songs possibly serve to keep members of the groups together while they make their long transoceanic migrations.

Locusts, or migratory short-horned grasshoppers, are generally not social. But once every four to six years a generation of locusts swarms. Huge clouds of them fill the sky periodically in India, Africa, and the Middle East. They land on a green field and leave it bare a short time later. Because of the harm locusts do, many scientists have studied this swarming habit. What makes billions of them fly together?

A favorable season with lots of food makes the locust population increase. If the next season is bad and food is scarce, the locusts are forced to crowd together.

Recent experiments show that the male locusts secrete a

a swarm of adult locusts

chemical over their body. When the males and females jostle together, this chemical stimulates the females to grow rapidly and lay eggs that develop in half the regular time. The locust eggs are laid in dense groups, so that the young, called nymphs, form small bands and are in very close contact when they hatch from the eggs. At first they are without wings. They spend days basking in the sunlight and crawl under stones or onto plants at night.

When the days get warm, migration starts. One band of nymphs may begin to march. It meets another and the two merge. This buildup continues until enormous bands of them are marching along together. Then they acquire wings. The locusts now start to fly, and the sight of one swarm flying makes another take off into the air too. Swarms keep joining until there are locusts enough to darken the sky with their wings.

Hibernating Together

With the approach of winter, crowds of animals may collect in favorable places and hibernate, that is, go into a deep sleep in which the rate of all life functions is slowed down to a minimum.

Ladybugs gather by the thousands in cracks of rocks and trees or in other protected places. In one such place a scientist found 9808 beetles lying one on top of the other. When cold weather comes, snakes follow each other's trails to holes in warm protected areas and intertwine their bodies, forming huge balls of snakes. Earthworms migrate down into the earth and hibernate, dozens together, in closely packed balls. Bats hibernate in immense numbers in dark caves.

This social habit of congregating during hibernation gives added protection to the members of the group. It keeps the temperature from getting too low and helps to preserve moisture.

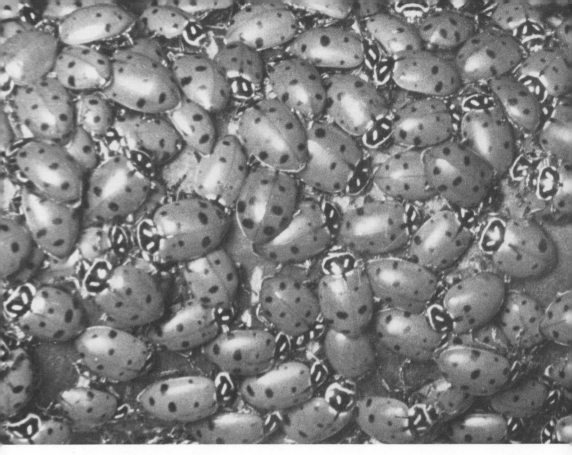

ladybugs hibernating together

Breeding Together

On islands, rocky cliffs, sandy dunes, and even on icy plains, birds gather in huge colonies to breed. A few of these colonies have been observed by biologists. To the casual onlooker, they may appear to be merely disorderly crowds of birds. Patience and perseverance are needed to find out what really goes on in such groups.

For several years Niko Tinbergen watched the breeding colonies of herring gulls and marked as many birds as possible with colored leg rings. He also learned to recognize certain small differences in the appearance of the birds, so that he and his co-workers were able to follow some of the gulls from day to day throughout the breeding season and during the several years of the study. At first he watched the colony through binoculars from a high dune far enough away so that the gulls did not mind his presence. Gradually he came nearer. For close observation, he hid in a hide and looked out through a hole.

During the winter the breeding grounds are deserted. But on a warm sunny day in March the sky above the breeding grounds suddenly fills with soaring, circling gulls. Finally they sweep out of sight again. This behavior is re-

herring gulls

peated for many days until the whole flock comes down and takes possession. At first the groupings look hit-and-miss, but in a few minutes most of the gulls separate into couples. These birds are older ones that paired off the past year or years and found each other weeks before the first visit to the dune. Herring gulls mate for life, and although they separate after breeding they come together again each spring.

Most of the birds stand in couples, but in certain parts of the breeding grounds some stand in larger groups. These groups are clubs of younger birds, and in them young gulls first select their mates.

The curious thing about the colony is that although many hundreds of birds are gathered together, each couple has a little area around its nest that becomes its own private territory. Here the two mates will take care of their eggs and young, and they will drive away intruders. If another gull moves into this particular area, the male of the couple usually charges at it, half running, half flying, until the intruder flies away. At the boundary of the territories between two neighbors there are frequent clashes. It is as though *No Trespassing* signs go up all over the colony around each mated pair and its nest area.

The individual couples are separate in their territories, yet they are still a part of a social community. If a person approaches a gull colony, one gull will stop feeding, crane its neck, and look at him. The other gulls nearby immediately do the same. One gull gives the alarm call, *Hahaha!* The others all echo it, and soon hundreds of gulls take off into the air together. Instead of flying away, the screaming gulls may gather above an intruder and swoop down on him again and again, hitting him with their feet. The gull-colony members cooperate in a social way to defend themselves against attack.

Another biologist, Bernard Stonehouse, spent weeks in the cold winter of the Antarctic studying the breeding colonies of the emperor penguins. In the middle of the cold, dark winter the emperors gather to breed on icy fields swept by gales and snowstorms. The average temperature is from

emperor penguins

thirteen degrees below zero Fahrenheit to thirty-one degrees below zero.

There are couples here too, but they do not fiercely defend the territory around their nest. Instead they tend to stand together in close groups. As a matter of fact, the "nest" is on the foot of the emperor penguin, where the egg is held and thus kept off the icy ground. A special fold of skin hangs over the egg like a curtain and helps to keep it warm. As soon as the egg is laid, the mother emperor leaves it on the foot of the father penguin and moves out to open water to feed. The male incubates the egg for sixty days, during which time he fasts completely. At the end of this time the female returns and takes over the feeding of the newly hatched chick.

A peculiar characteristic of the emperor penguin is that every adult has a drive to possess an egg and nurse a chick. Quite a number of the adults do not have their own chick, and so if any egg or chick is left momentarily by the parent, those that have no young press and push trying to get the chick or egg onto their own feet. There is often such a scramble that the egg is crushed and the young penguin trampled. Although it sometimes leads to trouble, this interest in the eggs and young by all adult birds is a social advance over the gull colony, where only the parent birds care for their eggs and young.

The young emperor penguins also have more of a social life than gulls do. When they are about five weeks old they gather in nursery groups, even though they continue to be fed by their parents.

When a storm comes there is real social cooperation. The adults surround the young birds and form a tight, compact group around them. All the adults face the center, with their beak resting on the shoulders of the bird in front. The birds on the outside always try to move toward the middle, so there is some place shifting. But the important thing is that the colony is meeting the blizzard as a solid mass, exposing only the smallest possible area of their bodies to the storm and completely protecting the chicks in the center. This cooperative action in the emperor-penguin colony helps to adapt it to the severe Antarctic climate.

·3·

Peck Orders in Birds

An observer watching a flock of chickens sometimes has a hard time, for all the chickens may look alike to him. But if he puts leg rings on them, he can tell them apart and begin to distinguish each member of the flock individually. He will then find that the birds know each other quite well and, in fact, live in a definite social order.

This finding is the amazing result of a study first made by a Norwegian psychologist, T. Schjelderup-Ebbe. He noticed that no hens could stay together long without establishing which was superior. They did so by fighting—pecking each other until one gave in. Sometimes no real fight took place, because one hen surrendered at the threat of a fight. But before long, in any group of hens, a real social order was established. The top hen dominated all the others and could peck any member of the flock without being pecked back. Second in line was a hen that pecked all the others except the top hen. A third hen pecked all those below her, and so on down until the peck order ended in a poor hen that was pecked by all and could peck no other in return.

Baby chicks did not peck each other at first, but as they grew older fighting began. Certain chicks learned to give in to others, and a full peck order was established by the time the chicks were ten weeks old.

Birds high in the peck order have first chance at food and the best choice of roosting places and nest boxes. They strut around proudly. The low-ranking members, on the other hand, have a submissive look. They are leaner, their heads are held lower, and their body feathers are ruffled.

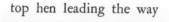
top hen leading the way

They show signs of fear and spend much of their time in out-of-the-way places. They have to feed after the top-ranking hens have fed or when their superiors are sleeping or otherwise busy.

Roosters have their own peck order when they are kept together. When put with hens, they dominate, but do not peck them. The top-ranking roosters mate more than roosters low in rank; one experiment showed that they fathered a lot more chicks than any of the others.

The fact that males usually dominate females led to the idea that if the male sex hormone were injected into low-ranking hens they would rise in the peck order. To test this theory, *testosterone*, the male hormone, was injected into white Leghorn hens. Results were as expected. The low-ranking hens became more aggressive and started to peck more, and in this way, they climbed the social ladder.

What purpose, if any, does the peck order serve in the life of chickens? To try to answer this question, an experiment was set up to compare two different flocks. One had a stable peck order. The other flock was kept from establishing the peck order by frequent shifts—every two days the hen longest present was replaced by a total stranger. Results showed that in the stable flock the chickens ate more, gained more weight, laid more eggs, and had many less wounds than those in the shifting flock. The social organization of chickens gave definite advantages to the group. It reduced fighting, made flock life more peaceful,

pigeons

and kept the members of the flock in a better state of health.

When the peck order was found among chickens, the discovery led to a series of new studies on the social life of other birds. Flocks of pigeons were studied. First they were observed in groups of separate sexes. In an all-female flock or an all-male flock, dominant birds pecked others lower in the social order—but curiously these lower birds often pecked back. The dominant birds did not win every time, but they won a majority of the fights. There is a definite dominance order in pigeon flocks, but it is not as hard and fast as that of chickens.

In a flock containing both sexes, male and female pigeons come together and mate. Each pair of birds then picks out a nest area and defends it against other members of the flock. Now a peculiar change comes over the pigeons. Even those that were subservient in the separate flocks become very aggressive and dominant around their territory, and they tend to win in any battles with newcomers. If one pair of pigeons is put into an empty pen that has room for fifty pairs, they immediately take over the entire area, and a second couple must fight them for a place. When a third couple arrives, both pairs of early settlers join to fight the newcomers. This behavior takes place every time a new pair is introduced. The latecomers have a difficult time, for they must battle all the others. Most birds change status in their society when the breeding season starts and there is a territory to be defended.

Canaries and parakeets have a social order similar to that of pigeons. There is dominance, but much more give and take between the dominant and subordinate members of the flock. When the breeding season arrives, home territory becomes important to these birds, too. A canary may be low in rank when it is on the neutral ground around the feeding trays, but in its own territory it can beat any new bird that comes along.

Male and female parakeets are hard to tell apart by their looks, but an observer can determine which is which by the way they act. When they are not breeding, the females

parakeets

dominate the males. The first birds to come to the feeding place are males. They take a few mouthfuls, and then other birds chase them away. They are the females. After the females eat their fill, the males are allowed to return for more food. When the breeding season comes, however, things are changed. The males become dominant and chase the females around.

Chickens, pigeons, canaries, and parakeets are all domesticated birds, but studies of wild birds show that many of them also have peck orders.

A remarkable thing was discovered when mixed flocks of

birds were studied. One such flock was made up of ninety-two birds—forty-two geese and fifty ducks. There were different kinds of geese and ducks in the group. There were Canada geese, blue geese, and snow geese. There were mallard ducks, wood ducks, scaup ducks, and a few others. The exciting new discovery was that these different kinds of birds lived in a definite social order. The blue geese dominated the Canada geese, which dominated the snow geese. All the geese dominated the ducks. But among the ducks there was a definite order too. Mallards dominated the wood ducks, which dominated the scaups. This order was clearly visible, especially when the birds were feeding.

Like the dominance orders in flocks of only one kind of bird, dominance in mixed flocks reduces fighting and makes for peaceful living.

·4·

The Social Life
of Mammals

All mammals feed their young with milk produced by mammary glands. For this reason all mammals take care of their babies during the nursing period, which may last for only a short time or for several years.

The young may be cared for in families having only one mother and father. Or they may be nursed by their mothers in mother herds, which the males join only in the mating season. Or the social group may be a clan in which males, females, and their young live together in a loose group. Some few mammals live in large communities that share a social life. These groupings are not hard and fast, and they often overlap. In some groups there is a social order like the peck orders among chickens; in others there is no such thing.

Families

Families in which one mother and father stay together to bring up the young year after year are rare among mammals. However, some animals are exceptions.

There are many stories about beaver life, and most of them come from American Indians, fur trappers, and hunters. But recently a planned piece of research on beaver life

mother beaver with two-week-old kits

was carried out in Michigan by a scientist named G. W. Bradt. He had a difficult time, for ponds and streams inhabited by beavers are often located far away from trails, and there are usually swamps and thickets surrounding them. Also, much of the beaver's life takes place behind the mud and sticks of its dam, and most of its activity goes on at night.

Beavers look alike, so Bradt had to catch the animals, determine their sex, and mark them. He did so by setting a trap behind a torn-away section of the dam. A break in a dam is a stimulus for a beaver to do repair work, so night after night beavers approached to mend the break. Finally all the members of the colony were taken, branded on the tail, and then released.

Bradt found out that a beaver colony is made up of a family—a mother, a father, and the young they produce. Each year beaver mothers give birth to three or four babies, which stay with the mother for two years. Then the two-year-olds leave or are driven out. So the average beaver family consists of the two parents, the beavers born the year before (yearlings), and the new babies (kits). When the two-year-olds are evicted, they look for mates and start their own lodges in the same pond, or they migrate to other ponds and streams if the pond is already overcrowded. There are usually about three separate lodges in a pond, but in some large ponds there may be as many as eight. Each lodge is occupied by one family only, all the members

timber wolves

of which cooperate to maintain the dams and do the other work of the colony.

A pack of wolves was once thought to consist of only two parents and their offspring, but recent work shows that many packs have several extra adults that may also breed.

There are usually about six baby wolves in a litter. The mother nurses them in the den until they are seven to eight weeks old. The pups are in constant contact with each other from birth, and from the twentieth day on they are in contact with adults too. In this way they form strong social attachments to members of the pack in the first few months of life. The pups leave the den between eight and ten weeks and afterward are fed by the parents as well as other adults. When they are seven months old, they may travel with the pack. By the time the pups are one year old, one female in the pack has another litter but the year-old pups stay on with their parents. A new pack is formed when a mated pair leaves the group to produce a litter of their own.

Several studies show that there are high-ranking, middle-ranking, and low-ranking wolves in any group. Two dominance orders exist: one among the males, the other among the females. The dominant wolves have first access to food, the best resting places, and are usually the ones who chase intruders away. A dominant male or female wolf also often leads the chase.

The average number of wolves in a pack is seven.

The gibbon is a small anthropoid (manlike) ape, with long arms, adapted to life in the trees. Dr. C. R. Carpenter spent months in the forests of northern Thailand studying its social life.

In the early morning the forest rang with the cries of the gibbons, and Dr. Carpenter located them by these sounds. Then he took his place behind a tree or other shelter so as not to disturb the apes. At 5:30 A.M. the gibbon troop

gibbon family

went to look for a good place to eat. The forest was loaded with fruits, fresh sweet buds, and succulent green leaves. The gibbons only had to move to a desirable tree and use their long arms to gather the food around them. They feasted for about two hours; then they all took a siesta. In the early afternoon they went to look for another food tree, and finally they moved to a tree in which they settled down for the night.

The gibbon troop varied from two to six individuals. Dr. Carpenter soon realized that it was a family group of a mother, a father, and their young. The pair have one offspring at a time, and this infant gibbon develops slowly and clings to its mother for the first six months of its life. Older offspring stay with the mother and father until they are mature enough to mate. Then they leave the family group. Each family has a territory of its own in the forest and defends it against other gibbon families. But this defense is mostly a battle of voices. When one family meets another, the two groups scream at each other until one group gives up and retreats. A complex system of signs, signals, and calls coordinates the activities of each family group.

Orangutans live in tropical rain forests in Borneo and Sumatra. The long red-haired male was often called the Old Man of the Forest. Little was known about these apes until recently when several scientists tracked the orangutans through the forest. They found that they live almost entirely

orangutan

in the trees and use their long arms to move through the branches of the tall trees in the rain forest. They eat fruit mostly but also feed on leaves, bark, and sometimes bird's eggs. But most importantly, the scientists were able to find out that the basic group is the female and her offspring and there are usually no more than four in a group. The male joins the group only to mate with the female and the rest of the time wanders alone.

Herds

Deer, sheep, goats, cattle, and horses belong to the group of animals with hoofs (ungulates). These animals graze on grass or other green vegetation and travel in herds from place to place by walking or running. Newborn calves, lambs, and colts are generally on their feet a short time after birth.

For many of these herd animals the most important social relation is between the mother and her offspring. Much of the year the mothers and their calves stay in separate herds. The males join them only to find mates, and after mating they either live alone or in herds of males.

The newborn lamb stays close to its mother and is constantly called to her side to nurse. After about ten days, the lamb runs at her side and follows her wherever she goes. The mother still tends to follow her own mother, and her mother follows *her* mother, and so on up to the oldest female in the flock, the leader.

A British naturalist, F. Fraser Darling, spent two years stalking and watching the red deer in the Scottish Highlands. As a result of his brilliant field study, he has given us the inside story of their social life. They have separate herds of females, called hinds, and usually the oldest is the leader. She is leader in the sense that she is the most

red deer, stags and hinds

watchful and alert member of the herd and is usually the first to give an alarm in case of danger. She is assisted by a second hind, which takes a rear position whenever the herd moves.

The stag herds are loosely organized; there is no definite leadership. Toward autumn the sex glands of the stag begin to enlarge, its neck grows thicker, and it gets a loud roaring voice. The rut, or mating, period starts around the end of September, and the stags trot toward the herds of hinds. The first stag that arrives starts off by claiming the whole herd as his harem, but then the other stags arrive and there is much roaring and fighting. Finally each stag settles down to about ten hinds. Even during the rut period when the stags dominate the hinds, the real leadership stays with the oldest female in the herd. If there is danger, she takes over and leads the various harem groups to safety. The stags may run with the group or go off by themselves. After mating, the sex groups separate again for the rest of the year.

The following June and July the calves are born. In five days the calf is up on its legs and able to follow its mother. The whole social organization is based on the mutual attachment of the mother and her young. The mothers are the real leaders of the group in these matriarchal animal societies.

Mothers are also the leaders of the group in elephant societies. In the late 1960's, Iain Douglas-Hamilton studied elephants in Tanzania, Africa, for four and a half years. During this time he came to recognize 414 of the 500 elephants that lived in Lake Manyera National Park!

The basic unit is a herd of ten to twenty females and their offspring, and it is led by the oldest, largest, and strongest female. The other females in the group are generally her daughters and granddaughters. The young male offspring stay until they are thirteen years old; then they are chased away and begin to live alone or in loose male groups. They join the family group for a short time again when they are ready to mate. Sometimes a small group of females

herd of elephants

and their calves will split off from the main group and form the beginning of another unit.

The members of the herd cooperate in many ways. Young calves can be nursed by any nursing females in the group. Often young females act as "aunts." That is, they help the mother take care of the offspring.

If a young elephant falls when hit by a dart or a gun, the others rush to help it to its feet. Also, the matriarch takes the most forward position when danger threatens and is the

young elephants greeting each other

last to retreat. In a dangerous situation, the herd gathers in a tight group behind her while the calves squeeze in between and underneath the adults.

During the breeding season the herds of females and young are attended by the males that have joined the group.

Zebras live in stable groups too, but in their case an adult stallion stays with the herd all through the year and defends his harem of females against other males. He usually has about six females, which with their young make up an average herd size of fifteen members. The oldest female leads the group to feeding areas and sleeping places. But when the zebras are attacked, the male stallion brings up the rear and tries to kick and butt the attackers while the herd runs away. If one of the group is separated from the rest, the others will search for it. Sometimes the small herds join together

herd of zebras

into large herds when they are attracted to the same good feeding area.

Troops

Baboons, which are natives of Africa, are large ground-living monkeys with doglike faces. They live in troops ranging in size from ten to several hundred members. The average number is forty of which six are males, twelve are females, and about twenty-four are infants and young.

Each troop has its own territory and is familiar with its good feeding spots, water holes, and safe sleeping places. At dawn the troop moves down from its rocky ledge or sleeping tree to places where there are prickly pears, berries, bulbs, roots, and bees' nests or other insects to feed on. They spend most of their time eating, resting, or picking dirt and parasites from each other's fur. This grooming helps to keep friendly relations in the group.

There is a dominance order in a troop of baboons, which can be seen when members of the troop move past each other. The less dominant animal always gets out of the way of the more dominant one. Dominant males hold the highest rank and take the best feeding and resting places, receive the most grooming from other members, and mate with the most females.

Strong social bonds run all through the troop. Males are attracted to the females only when they are ready to mate. Babies are dependent and cling to their mothers from the

two female baboons and young

day they are born. All the members of the troop are attracted to infants and often form groups around a mother
and her baby. As the young baboon grows, it gradually
starts to leave its mother and plays with other baby baboons.

Females have friendship groups with several other females. Even the dominant males associate together in small groups. All these interrelations bind the troop together into a social unit.

When the troop moves along, and it can cover several miles in a day, the females with infants, the younger baboons, and the most dominant males are in the center of the troop. In the back and front are the less dominant males. This arrangement keeps females and young protected on all sides by the adult males. There are other protective advantages to the group too. There are more eyes to perceive danger and more voices to give warning calls. There are more searchers for good feeding and sleeping places. And there is always a monkey handy to keep another's fur clean. For all of these reasons, group life among baboons helps them to survive in competition with other animals. Scientists who have watched baboons in their natural environment say that a baboon without its troop cannot survive for long.

Other kinds of monkeys have different social patterns. A lot is known about howling monkeys, which are noted for their unusual voices. Dr. C. R. Carpenter, who studied the gibbons, also spent two years watching howlers, in the hot rain forest on the island of Barro Colorado in the Panama Canal Zone.

Groups of howling monkeys move through the trees every day, feeding on fresh fruits, young buds, and leaves.

By watching many such groups, Dr. Carpenter found that they usually have eighteen members. Of the eighteen, about three are males, about eight are females, and the rest are infants and young monkeys. There is no dominance order. Each member of the group is equal to the others. The adult males share the females and also cooperate in leading the way through the forest and in defending the group. Like many other monkeys, howlers spend most of their time feeding and resting. They, too, have their own territories in the forest and defend them against other clans—mostly by voice battles. Vocal signals also help to keep members

red howlers

of the troop together when they travel through the forest. In general, life within the howling-monkey troops is peaceful and cooperative.

We have learned a lot about chimpanzees in zoos and laboratories, but there were practically no field reports on their social life until 1931 when a biologist named Dr. Henry Nissen followed chimpanzees through the deep tangled forests of Guinea for more than two months.

Nothing much happened until the 1960's when three field studies were made in three different areas of East and Central Africa. Adriaan Kortlandt studied chimpanzees on a plantation in the eastern Congo. Vernon and Frances Reynolds in 1962 studied chimpanzees in the Budongo Forest of Uganda, and recently Jane Goodall did a six-year study of wild populations of chimpanzees on the shores of Lake Tanganyika. Her technique was to make herself visible in the area where chimpanzees lived until they finally became used to her. Eventually she got to know each member of a group of chimpanzees that came every day to eat bananas at her camp and she followed them through the forest as well.

A team of Japanese scientists from Kyoto University also studied wild populations of chimpanzees in Tanzania.

Chimpanzees have a home range of about ten square miles, where they stay from year to year. In this area they wander from place to place, looking for food and sleeping in a different place each night. A typical day in the life of

mother chimpanzee with juvenile and infant

chimpanzees is like that of other monkeys and apes. They
get up at dawn, feed for a few hours, rest, move on, feed
again, and at night take shelter in a tree.

About thirty to eighty chimpanzees live in the same home

range, but the entire group is hardly ever seen together. Usually two or three chimpanzees move in a group, although these units form and re-form constantly. A particular chimpanzee might be in a certain group one day and in another the next.

The permanent relations are between mothers and their young. The newborn chimp is a helpless little thing and is carried around by the mother all the time. It nurses when it is hungry. After about five months, it starts to move away from the mother, take a little solid food, and walk a few steps. By the time it is a year old, it can run, jump, swing, and climb. But it stays close to its mother and nurses until it is almost three years old. Even then it stays close to its mother and does not become a fully mature adult until it is ten years old. Over this course of time it learns how to be an acceptable member of chimpanzee society.

Most of what has recently been learned about gorillas comes from the studies made by George Schaller and by Dian Fossey.

A troop of mountain gorillas numbers anywhere from two to thirty members with an average of about seventeen. The leader of the group is a fully adult silver-backed male (the hair on his back is silvery gray). There are usually two younger males whose hair is all black, six females, and seven or eight young ones, some of which are infants and others several years old.

The group wanders slowly through the forest in the early

troop of mountain gorillas

morning feeding on plants. They nibble on blossoms and leaves, yank young trees out by the roots, and chew on the branches. Some of their favorite plants are bamboo, wild celery, and wild bananas. They eat steadily for about two hours until their bellies are full. Then they take a rest from midmorning to midafternoon. But while the adults are resting, the young gorillas play. They run, climb, and swing on vines. Often they chase each other around and wrestle with each other. The silver-backed male determines when and where to rest and when to stop the rest period.

Usually the rest period is over by midafternoon, and the gorillas start to feed again. As the forest grows dark, they collect near the silver-backed male and start to build nests for the night as soon as he does. The nests are built either on the ground or in the trees.

In general, gorillas lead a peaceful life for they have few enemies (except men with guns). They are not at all the fearsome animals they were once thought to be, and if left alone are gentle.

Towns

One little rodent belonging to the ground-squirrel family is called a prairie dog. Its only resemblance to a dog is that it barks like one. It is interesting to us because it lives in "towns," and as a member of a large community it has patterns of behavior that are very different from those of other animals.

Dr. John A. King camped among the prairie dogs in a national-park refuge in the Black Hills of South Dakota and for two years studied their ways. As a result of his studies, we now know much about their social life.

A large prairie-dog town may occupy seventy-five acres and have nearly a thousand members. It looks like a unit, but actually it is divided into separate little territories, each claimed by a prairie-dog clan, or coterie, of about ten mem-

young prairie dogs at their burrows

bers. The coterie is the basic unit of the town. It is comparable to one household in a large village. Its members share burrows and constantly greet one another with friendly acts. Prairie dogs from other coteries are treated as enemies. If two coterie members meet, they turn their heads toward each other, open their mouths, bare their teeth, and "kiss." This kiss serves to tell friend from foe, for only members of the same coterie will share kisses. Members of another coterie will run away or fight.

A young prairie dog emerging for the first time from its burrow meets the friendly members of its own coterie, which accept it as their own and kiss and groom it just as its mother does. As it grows and begins to wander, it learns to recognize the boundary of its territory and finds that members of other coteries do not treat it well.

The only time there is cooperation among the members of different coteries is when warning cries are given upon the approach of danger. The prairie dogs all sit up when they hear such a cry, and if it is continued they dash into their burrows. With this exception, the coterie lives its own life within the large town.

All this research shows that mammals have very different ways of living together. Their social habits are dependent on several factors—the kind of mammal they are, the length of time it takes for the young to grow up, and the social forms that have best protected these different animals in their past history on the Earth.

Other Social Groups

Lions live in social groups known as prides. There are usually about fifteen lions in a pride. About seven of them

pride of lions

are females that have grown up together. Usually two are
males. The rest are cubs and other young lions in the
process of growing up. The females lead the group from
one place to another and do most of the killing of prey.
When hunting, the females stalk the prey cooperatively.
They fan out and then rush in from different directions.
When the prey is caught, the males move in and push the
females and cubs away. They eat their fill and, when satis-
fied, allow the others to have a share. Young male adoles-
cents are driven from the pride and form their own groups
or wander alone. When they get a chance, they attach themselves to a new pride, although they may have to fight the
resident males first.

The harems of Alaska fur seals, which form in late

Alaska fur seals

spring, are especially large. As the breeding season approaches male seals, or bulls, weighing about 600 pounds each, heave themselves up onto the shores of the Pribilof Islands. These islands lie in the Bering Sea between Alaska and Siberia. The bulls establish territories on the barren rocky shores and await the coming of the cows. The best territories are near the water's edge, for when the females arrive the bulls nearest the water will have first choice. The females appear in the middle of June, together with young males that are not yet ready to breed.

The first cow to arrive is claimed by the nearest bull. The next cows seem to want company, for they usually join the first cow. So the lucky bull that got the first one soon accumulates a large harem. But he has to fight to keep his harem intact, since more and more cows keep coming in and other bulls start to collect their harems. Within a few days, the females bear their pups, conceived the year before on the same islands. About a week later they come into heat and are ready to mate with the bulls.

Throughout the mating season the bulls dominate the females in their harems, herding them into tight groups from which they cannot easily escape or be carried away by other bulls, which are always ready to snatch a cow. Once in a while a fight breaks out. Then there is a great roaring and bellowing, and one bull lunges at the other and perhaps seriously wounds him. Through all of this commotion, the mother seal nurses her young with her milk. She feeds the pup steadily for six days; then she goes to sea to feed, coming back only one day a week to allow her pup to nurse.

A few days after birth the young pups join into groups called pods. After a few weeks the pods of pups go down to the sea together and take their first jump into the water. They soon learn to swim and spend the next weeks playing in the water. When the days grow colder, both young and old put out to the open sea. The males remain close to the Bering Sea, but the females and young may travel over 3000 miles in the north Pacific Ocean. The following summer they return to the Pribilof Islands for their short but important social season on land.

·5·

Insect Societies

In American pioneer days families who ventured west had to provide everything for themselves. The man of the family cut down trees to build a home. He trapped food, and with the help of his wife and children cleared the land and planted the seeds of wheat, corn, and vegetables. The woman of the family wove the cloth, made the clothes, ground the wheat and corn, and baked the bread.

Our town and city societies of today are much more complicated. We rely on farmers in outlying areas for our plant food. We buy meat cut from cattle that farmers send to the packing houses. Manufacturers provide us with clothes, shoes, and thousands of other articles. We live in a society in which jobs are specialized.

It is just because our society is so complicated that we wonder at the lowly insects, some of which have communities that seem almost as complex. We know the amount and kinds of things we need, and we know that they can be produced only by a division of labor. But how do insects, with such tiny brains, organize their activities for the good of the colony? How do thousands of bees or ants live together, some building the nest, others bringing in food, still others caring for the young or defending the nest, so that all the duties necessary for the continued life of the colony are carried out?

We have marveled at insect societies for a long time. But new experimental studies have been made that show us how amazing their ways of cooperating really are.

Honeybees

Watch a beehive, and you will see bees taking off one after another from its entrance, and others streaming in from the fields and orchards. These bees are the foragers that are finding food for the whole colony. They go to the flowers that are filled with nectar and pollen, and they return to the hive and pass the food to the house bees.

The house bees in turn give the nectar to other members of the colony, which store it in special cells where it is evaporated into honey. Some of the foragers deposit

swarm of honeybees

pollen in certain cells, and house bees immediately ram this pollen into a tight lump in the cell. The honey and pollen are the basic food stores of the colony. All the adult bees partake of it, and some of them feed it to the young bees that are developing in special cells.

The work of the colony has much to do with food. But there is also water to be collected. There are comb cells of wax to be built, and cells to be cleaned and prepared for eggs. The hive must be ventilated and its temperature regulated. The entrance to the hive has to be guarded against enemies. These jobs are done by sexless females called worker bees, which make up 99 percent of the colony. The other 1 percent is made up of several hundred drones, the males, and the mother of the colony, the queen bee—a fertile female that lays all the eggs.

There may be 20,000 to 80,000 workers in a nest, and every once in a while the population gets so big that there is no longer room for the growing brood. Then the colony divides, or swarms. Crowds of bees rush out and rise into the air. The old queen appears and leaves the hive with the swarming bees.

Meanwhile, in the old colony, virgin queens are developing in special "royal" cells. The drones now leave the colony and join swarms of males from other nests nearby. When one of the new virgin queens emerges, she emits a special "queen" chemical substance into the air. It attracts the males in the area, and one of them reaches her in mid-air and fertilizes her. He dies soon afterward. But the queen makes a few flights a day for several days, and on each flight mates with a different male. She now has within her enough sperm to fertilize all the eggs she will lay for the rest of her life. She then either returns to the nest and destroys any other virgin queens that may have developed, or else she swarms with a group of workers to a new nesting cavity.

Instantly she is surrounded by worker bees. In a few days she begins to deposit eggs one by one in the empty cells of the combs. She may lay 2000 eggs per day, 200,000

queen bee surrounded by drones

in a season, and during her lifetime of about five years up to 1,000,000 eggs. The eggs hatch into little legless grubs called larvae. They are fed by worker bees, and then grow and change into pupae, a resting stage from which they emerge as perfect full-sized bees.

Day after day hundreds of worker bees emerge from cells in the hive and take their place in bee society. Each does what is necessary for the life of the colony. No bee issues orders, yet all the work is done efficiently and the needs of the colony are taken care of. How does this happen? Does each bee hatch out as a particular kind—a forager, a builder of combs, or a nurse bee? Or is there some other way in which bee activities are organized?

A German experimenter, G. A. Rösch, watched marked bees in a glass-walled observation hive and came to the conclusion that the duties of a worker bee change with its age. He observed that during the five- to six-week lifetime of the worker bee it followed a succession of jobs. The newly emerged worker cleaned out brood cells for about three days. Then it became a nurse bee and fed pollen and honey to the older larvae. At six days it developed special nursing glands that produced bee milk, or royal jelly, a special protein-rich food. It was noticed that royal jelly was fed to all larvae for the first three days of their lives, but afterward only the larvae in queen cells continued to receive it. At about twelve days, the worker bee developed glands that secrete wax, and it became a builder of comb

worker honeybees exchanging food

cells. From the sixteenth to the twentieth day, it began to receive the nectar and pollen brought by the foraging bees. On the twentieth day it stood guard at the entrance to the hive, and a few days later it shifted to its last and longest job—foraging, or flying out of the hive to collect nectar and pollen.

And so it appeared to Rösch that each worker bee went through a schedule of duties determined by its age. But he found that this schedule was not rigid. He took all the nursing bees away from a colony and left only foragers. Soon some of these foraging bees regenerated nursing glands and started to carry on nursing activities, even though they were well past the age for it. He deprived another colony of its foragers and left it with only young nursing bees. For two days no food was collected, but on the third day a few of the oldest bees (eight to twelve days old) flew out and brought back pollen and nectar, even though, according to their age, they were still nursing bees.

A big question remained. How does a worker bee find out what jobs need to be done? Another experimenter, Martin Lindauer, set out to answer this question. He watched a single marked bee from the first day of its life to its last. He found that on the whole the worker bee does stick to its schedule, but it can do many other jobs at the same time. The bee he watched spent a lot of time patrolling around the hive. It inspected old and new cells and the growing larvae. Each tour of inspection resulted in some form of activity, either nursing, cleaning, or building. Lindauer concluded that each bee finds out for itself what has to be done by its inspection tours.

In this way the worker bees become sensitive to the needs of the community as a whole, so the program changes in response to these needs. When the nest gets too warm, for instance, the bees first cool it by fanning their wings. But when it gets really hot, there is a striking change of behavior in the colony, and the principle of cooling by evaporation is used. The home bees, which do not collect water, first use the contents of their own honey stomachs as a water substitute. These contents are not pure honey, but a solution containing 60 percent water. The home bees regurgitate droplets of it over the comb cells. The water in the droplets evaporates and helps to cool the hive. Now the bees that have given up droplets from their stomachs begin to beg their nearest neighbors for water by tapping them with their antennae. This action spreads from the center of the overheated hive to the entrance. There the home bees rush up to the home-coming forager bees and beg for the contents of their honey stomachs. The nectar with a greater percentage of water comes to be in great demand, and soon some of the nectar collectors begin to collect plain water. In a short time load after load of water is brought to the nest and the nest is cooled. When the bees at the entrance slow down in their demands for water and the returning bees cannot dispose of their water loads quickly, they go back to collecting nectar from the flowers.

This collective sharing of food is the main tie that binds the members of the colony together and makes them sensitive to a surplus or deficit of ingredients in their food. As we have seen, the amount of water collected was controlled by the demand for water in the hive. In the same way the amount of pollen collected might be determined by the need for it. If pollen collectors find it difficult to deposit their loads, they might shift to other kinds of food collecting.

Much recent work on honeybees has to do with chemical substances known as pheromones. These substances are secreted by glands in the bee's body. When released, they make other bees respond in special ways. For example, over thirty chemical substances have been found in the head of the honeybee queen. We still do not know what all these substances control. But we do know that one of them prevents worker bees from building royal cells in which new queens are raised. As long as the queen bee secretes this substance and the worker bees lick it from her body and pass it through the hive, no rival queens develop. It also prevents worker bees from laying eggs. All eggs are thus laid by the queen only. But if the queen dies or disappears, this pheromone disappears too, and more queens are reared. Another pheromone makes the worker bees cluster around her in the hive and when she swarms to another nest.

One of the interesting discoveries made about bees is

that they are not as busy as we have always thought. Much of the time a bee just loafs. If it finds no work to perform it becomes motionless on the comb. Bees are not as efficient as we believed, either. One bee may put wax into the wall of a comb cell, and another worker may come along and take this same wax away. But in spite of individual loafing and inefficiency, the beehive as a whole is remarkably successful.

Ants

Ants were already social in their way of life forty million years ago. Today there is an ant population of about 5,000,000,000,000,000. They build nests in the wood of houses and trees. They tunnel into the earth and burrow into the stems of living plants. Some build nests of paper or leaves. Most live in colonies where the numbers range from a few to hundreds of thousands.

A new colony of ants starts its life with a marriage flight. On warm, moist days in the spring, summer, or autumn, ant colonies become very excited. Large numbers of ants rush around the entrance to the anthill. Some of them enlarge the entrance to the nest so that the female queens and the males can emerge from the nest. Both are much bigger than the average ant and have delicate wings. At first a few of these royal couples come out, and then more and more of them appear at the entrance. The same excitement is taking place at the entrance to all the ant nests in the region.

colony of carpenter ants

Suddenly, as though a signal were given, all the queens and males of the many different colonies fly into the air. Their time of departure is actually determined by a certain temperature and humidity of the air. If you are outside at the time, you will see clouds of flying ants.

As bees do, the males catch the queens in midair and mate with them, and in this one mating the male supplies each queen with enough sperm to fertilize all the eggs she will ever lay. Then both males and females fall to the ground. The males die, but the queens live on. Each queen shakes or bites off her wings and finds a place to start a new colony.

Very soon the queen begins to lay her eggs. Larvae hatch out from them, and then they change into pupae, the resting stage from which they emerge as adult ants. Most of these new members of the colony-to-be are females like the queen, but they cannot lay eggs. Just as in the honeybee colony, these sexless females are the workers that do all the jobs of the colony except egg laying. The queen alone lays eggs, and she does nothing else for the rest of her life.

The worker ants now care for the new eggs, larvae, and pupae the queen produces, and soon there is a big ant community. A tremendous amount of work is done in the colony, and, like the bees, the ants divide this labor. Some worker ants go out to forage for food. Others tend the queen and carry off her newly laid eggs to special chambers. The larvae that hatch from these eggs are fed and licked to keep their skins moist. New ants ready to hatch out from their pupal skins must be helped to emerge. New chambers have to be built for the developing brood. Broken parts of the nests need to be repaired, and the nest must be kept clean and protected against enemies. Some kinds of ants have a special group of "soldiers" with large heads and powerful jaws, whose special function is to protect the colony.

Ants do not seem to have a schedule of work the way

queen carpenter ant (arrow) attended by nurse ants

bees do. But in general the young ants remain in the nest and care for the brood, while older ants go out on food-collecting expeditions. Usually the inside group does not take up outside work, and vice versa. But experiments have shown that ants, too, can change their occupations when the needs of the colony change. Certain ant nests were provided with a brood of eggs, larvae, and pupae. Then only outside workers were put into the nest. At first the brood was completely neglected and many of them died.

But finally some ants began to care for the remaining eggs, and the colony survived.

All the ants in a colony are extremely sensitive to one another. The slightest movement on the part of one ant may lead its nestmates to imitate it. A young worker ant may just look on at first when it comes across a group working. But then it runs along with the group, and soon afterward joins in with whatever job the group is doing.

If one ant discovers a large amount of food, it gets very excited and manages to excite all the other ants it meets. The excited ant taps the others with its antennae or pecks at various parts of their bodies. Soon many ants rush out of the nest to find the food site.

They are able to do so because the ant that found the food laid a chemical trail on its way back to the nest. The chemical comes out of a tube at the back end of the ant's body. As the ant runs back to the nest it stops often and presses its body against the ground, leaving a spot of the chemical. When the other ants emerge from the nest, they follow this trail. This "food-trail" chemical is just one of the many pheromones that have been discovered in ants.

When ants are disturbed, they give off a special "alarm" pheromone. Ants nearby either run to where the disturbance occurred, or they scatter in all directions while they try to rescue their eggs and larvae.

Another clue to the way the work of the ant colony is coordinated comes from the feeding of one ant by another.

Some of the food a worker ant collects outside the nest stays in its crop, a first stomach that functions as a storage organ. When the ant reaches the nest, it is met by a hungry ant, which begs for food by tapping the other with its antennae. Both ants then raise themselves high up on their legs with their heads together, and the foraging ant pumps liquid food from its crop into the begging ant's mouth. One experimenter showed how widespread this food sharing is. He fed honey that had been stained blue to six yellow ants. Within twenty-four hours the whole colony showed the blue stain inside their bodies.

Besides sharing food, ants constantly touch one another with their antennae, licking and cleaning one another's bodies. In this way all the chemical "news" of the colony is passed from one ant to the next.

Harmony of action in the ant community seems to be based on food sharing, the constant close contact between the members of the colony, their extreme sensitivity to the slightest movement in other ants, and most of all to the chemical pheromones that are constantly being passed around.

The variety that has been found in animal societies is amazing. How could it have come about? The answer lies in the process of natural selection.

Many social groups have arisen over and over again among the ancestors of modern animals. Social behavior that was bad for the members of the society did not last but died out with the animals that practiced it.

Those social groups that have survived are the ones that protect their members from enemies and help them to find food. All the animals on Earth today have ways of living that give them some advantage in the struggle for life.

Bibliography

(P) means paperback

Allee, W. C. *The Social Life of Animals.* Beacon Press, Boston, 1958. (P)

Alverdes, Friedrich. *Social Life in the Animal World.* Harcourt Brace, New York, 1927.

Baumgartel, Walter. *Up Among the Mountain Gorillas.* Hawthorn Books, New York, 1976.

Bonner, J. T. *Cells and Societies.* Princeton University Press, Princeton, New Jersey, 1955.

Bourlière, François. *The Natural History of Mammals.* A. A. Knopf, New York, 1954.

Darling, Frank F. *A Herd of Red Deer: A Study in Animal Behavior.* Oxford University Press, New York, 1937.

DeVore, B. I., ed. *Primate Behavior.* Holt, Rinehart & Winston, New York, 1965.

89

Douglas-Hamilton, I. & O. *Among the Elephants,* Viking, New York, 1975.

Freeman, Dan. *The Love of Monkeys and Apes.* Octopus Books Ltd., London, 1977.

Frisch, Karl von. *The Dancing Bees.* Harvest, New York, 1961. (P)

Goetsch, Wilhelm. *The Ants.* University of Michigan Press, Ann Arbor, Michigan, 1957. (P)

Goodall, Jane. *In the Shadow of Man.* Houghton Mifflin, Boston, 1971.

——— *My Friends the Wild Chimpanzees.* National Geographic Society, Washington, D.C., 1967.

Hediger, H. *Wild Animals in Captivity.* Academic Press, New York, 1950.

Lindauer, Martin. *Communication Among Social Bees.* Harvard University Press, Cambridge, Massachusetts, 1961.

MacClintock, Dorcas. *A Natural History of Zebras.* Charles Scribner's Sons, New York, 1976.

Marler, P. R. *The Marvels of Animal Behavior.* National Geographic Society, Washington, D.C., 1972.

Mech, David L. *The Wolf.* Natural History Press, New York, 1970.

Michener, Charles D. and Michener, Mary H. *American Social Insects.* Van Nostrand, Princeton, New Jersey, 1951.

Morley, Derek W. *The Ant World.* Penguin Books, Baltimore, 1953. (P)

Murchison, Carl A., ed. *Handbook of Social Psychology.* Clark University Press, Worcester, Massachusetts, 1935.

Noble, Ruth C. *Nature of the Beast.* Doubleday, Garden City, New York, 1945.

Portmann, Adolf. *Animals as Social Beings.* Viking, New York, 1961.

Ribbands, C. Ronald. *Behavior and Social Life of Honeybees.* Dover, New York, 1957.

Richards, Owain W. *The Social Insects.* Harper Torchbooks, New York, 1961.

Schaller, G. B. *The Mountain Gorilla.* University of Chicago Press, Chicago, 1964.

——— *The Year of the Gorilla.* Ballantine Books, New York, 1965.

———— *Wonders of Lions*. Dodd, Mead Co., New York, 1977.

Scott, John P. *Animal Behavior*. University of Chicago Press, Chicago, 1958.

Sebeok, Thomas A., ed. *How Animals Communicate,* Indiana University Press, Bloomington, 1977.

Terres, John K. *The Wonders I See*. J. B. Lippincott, Philadelphia, 1960.

Tinbergen, Nikolaas. *The Herring Gull's World*. Basic Books, New York, 1961.

———— *Social Behavior in Animals*. Wiley, New York, 1953.

Wheeler, William M. *Social Life Among the Insects*. Harcourt Brace, New York, 1923.

Wilson, Edward O. *Sociobiology*. Harvard University Press, Cambridge, Massachusetts, 1975.

Young, Stanley P. and Goldman, Edward A. *The Wolves of North America*. American Wildlife Institute, Washington, D.C., 1944.

Zuckerman, S. *Social Life of Monkeys and Apes*. Harcourt Brace, New York, 1932.

Magazines such as *Scientific American, Natural History,* and *Audubon Magazine* often have articles on the social behavior of animals.

Index

indicates illustration

Allee, W. C., 14, 16
anthill, 82

birds, 9, 12, 19, 21, 22*, 24-28, 31-43, 45
  bobolinks, 26
  blackbirds, 26
  canaries, 41, 42
  chickens, 12, 37-40, 38*, 42, 45
  crows, 26
  ducks, 26, 43
  emperor penguins, 34*-36
  geese, 26, 43
  grackles, 24
  hawks, 19
  herring gulls, 31-34, 32*
  kingbirds, 26
  migration of, 26*-30, 27*, 29*
  mixed flocks of, 42, 43
  parakeets, 25, 41, 42*
  peck order of, 37-43, 38*
  pelicans, 21, 22*
  pigeons, 12, 22, 40*-42
  robins, 24
  starlings, 19, 21, 24, 25*
  waxwings, 26
Bradt, G. W., 46

breeding colonies, 31-36, 32*, 34*

Carpenter, Dr. C. R., 48, 50, 60, 61

Darling, F. Fraser, 52
Douglas-Hamilton, Ian, 10, 54

earthworms, 30

family groups, 45*-52, 49*
fish, 9, 15-19, 18*, 22
    goldfish, 16*, 17
    herring, 17
    jellyfish, 15
    mackerel, 17, 18*
    minnows, 17
    porpoises, 22
    schools of, 9, 17
Fossey, Dian, 64

Goodall, Jane, 10*, 62

herds, 52-58
hibernation, 30, 31*

insects, 9, 15, 21, 26-30, 29*, 31*, 58, 73-87, 75*, 77*, 78*, 83*, 85*
    ants, 21, 82-87, 83*, 85*
    bees, 74-82, 75*, 77*, 78*, 84, 85
    ladybug beetles, 30, 31*
    locusts, 28-30, 29*
    Mayflies, 15
    monarch butterflies, 26-28, 27*

termites, 21

King, John A., 66
Kortlandt, Adriaan, 62

Lindauer, Martin, 79, 80

mammals, 9-11*, 10*, 13, 20*, 21, 23*, 44-72, 45*, 53*, 55*, 56*, 59*, 61*, 63*, 65*, 67*, 69*
    Alaska fur seals, 69-72, 70*
    African wild dogs, 23*
    antelopes, 23
    apes, 9, 13, 48, 63
    baboons, 21, 58-60, 59*
    chimpanzees, 10*, 62-64, 63*
    deer, 9, 21, 52-54, 53*
    dolphins, 28
    elephants, 54-56*, 55*
    gazelles, 23
    gibbons, 45, 48-50, 49*
    goats, 52
    gorillas, 64-66, 65*
    horses, 52
    howling monkeys, 60-62, 61*
    hyenas, 23
    monkeys, 9, 13, 60, 61, 63
    musk oxen, 20*
    orangutans, 50, 51*
    prairie dogs, 66-68, 67*
    sheep, 13, 52
    whales, 19*, 20, 22, 23, **28**
    wolves, 9, 21, 23, 47*, 48
    zebras, 24, 56, 57*
migration, 26-30, 27*, 29*

Noctiluca, 15

paramecium, 15
peck orders, 37-43, 38*, 45
protozoa, 15

Rösch, G. A., 78, 79

Schaller, George, 10, 11*, 64
Schjelderup-Ebbe, T., 37
snakes, 30
Stonehouse, Bernard, 34

Tinbergen, Niko, 31

About the Author

Millicent E. Selsam's career has been closely connected with biology and botany. She majored in biology and was graduated *magna cum laude* with a B.A. degree from Brooklyn College. At Columbia she received her M.A. and M.Ph. in the Department of Botany. After teaching biology for ten years in the New York City high schools, she has devoted herself to writing. Ms. Selsam is the author of eighty-seven science books for children. She has received the Eva L. Gordon Award of the American Nature Study Society, the Thomas Alva Edison Award, two Boys Club of America awards, and the nonfiction award for the Total Body of Creative Writing given by the Washington Children's Book Guild in 1978. In addition, she is a fellow of the American Association for the Advancement of Science.

At present, Ms. Selsam lives in New York City and spends her summers on Fire Island, New York.